TUNDRA

ENDANGERED
BIOMES

DONNA LATHAM

Nomad Press
A division of Nomad Communications
10 9 8 7 6 5 4 3 2 1
Copyright © 2010 by Nomad Press

Printed by Regal Printing Limited in China,
June 2010, Job Number 1005019
ISBN: 978-1-934670-85-9

Questions regarding the ordering of this book should be addressed to
Independent Publishers Group
814 N. Franklin St.
Chicago, IL 60610
www.ipgbook.com

Nomad Press
2456 Christian St.
White River Junction, VT 05001
www.nomadpress.net

Image Credits

corbisimages.com/ Rolf Hicker, cover; Martin Harvey, 15, 16.

©iStockphoto.com/ Dmitry Deshevykh, i, 7, 20; Jan Rysavy, 1; Jussi
Santaniemi, 1; James Goldsworthy, 3; VisualCommunications, 5; Ray
Roper, 7; FokinOl, 7; Trevor Bauer, 8; TT, 9; Artem Illarionov, 11; Eric
Isselée, 11; VisualCommunications, 12, 14; Alexander Hafemann, 13,
15; chelovek, 13; Vladimir Gramagin, 13; Andrew Howe, 14; Stephen
Meese, 16; Phil Dickson, 17; tibu, 18; John Pitcher, 19; Jim Jurica, 21;
Jan Will, 22; Paul Tessier, 24; Tim McCaig, 25; Skip ODonnell, 26.

CONTENTS

chapter 1
What Is a Biome?—page 1

chapter 2
Landscape and Climate of the Tundra—page 3

chapter 3
Plants Growing in the Tundra
Have Adapted—page 7

chapter 4
Animals Living in the Tundra
Have Adapted—page 11

chapter 5
Environmental Threats—page 15

chapter 6
Biodiversity at Risk—page 19

chapter 7
The Future of the Tundra—page 23

chapter 8
Conservation Challenge—page 25

glossary • further investigations • index

What Is a Biome?

Grab your backpack! You're about to embark on an exciting expedition to explore one of the earth's major **biomes**: the tundra!

A biome is a large natural area with a distinctive **climate** and **geology**. The desert is a biome. The rainforest, ocean, and forest are also biomes. So is the tundra. Biomes are the earth's communities.

Did You Know?

Scientists don't agree on how many biomes there are. Some divide the earth into five biomes. Others argue for 12.

1

Words to Know

biome: a large natural area with a distinctive climate, geology, and set of water resources. A biome's plants and animals are adapted for life there.

climate: average weather patterns in an area over a period of many years.

geology: the rocks, minerals, and physical structure of an area.

adapt: changes a plant or animal makes to survive in new or different conditions.

ecosystem: a community of living and nonliving things and their environment. Living things are plants, animals, and insects. Nonliving things are soil, rocks, and water.

environment: everything in nature, living and nonliving.

Each biome has its own biodiversity, which is the range of living things **adapted** for life there. It also contains many **ecosystems**. In an ecosystem, living and nonliving things interact with their **environment**.

Teamwork keeps the system balanced and working. Earth's biomes are connected together, creating a vast web of life.

2

Landscape and Climate

You need to bundle up in the earth's coldest biome. Winters in the tundra are bitterly cold, with temperatures dropping to -40 degrees Fahrenheit (-40 degrees Celsius). Summers are cool, reaching only about 64 degrees Fahrenheit (18 degrees Celsius).

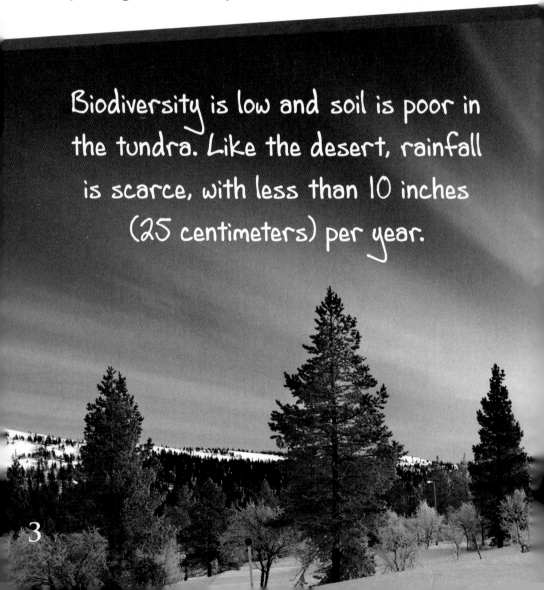

Biodiversity is low and soil is poor in the tundra. Like the desert, rainfall is scarce, with less than 10 inches (25 centimeters) per year.

of the Tundra

The tundra covers about 14 percent of Earth's landmass, mostly in the Arctic areas of Alaska, Canada, Greenland, and Siberia. These regions in the **Northern Hemisphere** are called the Arctic tundra.

High up on mountains, above the **timberline**, is the alpine tundra.

Although most of Antarctica is considered a cold desert, there is a stretch of tundra along Antarctica's coasts.

Words to Know

Northern Hemisphere: the half of the earth north of the equator.

timberline: also called the treeline. How far north or how high in the mountains trees grow.

4

The tundra has a layer of permanently frozen soil called permafrost. When the weather warms up in the summer, the very top layer of the permafrost thaws. This top layer is called the active layer. The rest remains frozen. It never defrosts.

Word Exploration

The word *tundra* comes from the Finnish word *tunturia*, which means "treeless plain."

When the active layer melts, it supplies a rich ecosystem for animals, plants, and insects. Then as winter approaches again, the active layer refreezes.

Plants Growing in the

Plants are the primary producers of the **food chain**. Without plants, animals can't survive.

But plants face many challenges in the tundra. Poor soil and little rainfall make for difficult conditions facing all plant life.

Through **adaptation**, plants have developed the right features to survive in their **habitats**. They live with the weather and make the most of their surroundings.

Words to Know

food chain: a community of animals and plants where each is eaten by another higher up in the chain.

adaptation: the development of physical or behavioral changes to survive in an environment.

habitat: a plant or animal's home.

global warming: the gradual warming of the planet, causing climate change.

climate change: a change in the world's weather and climate.

Tundra Have Adapted

A team of scientists in Norway has created a special storage vault in an Arctic mountain's permafrost. The vault stores a global food bank of 208,000 plant seeds. It's large enough to stockpile 2 billion of the world's seeds.

The idea is that permafrost will protect the earth's plants in case of disaster, such as disease, or the effects of continued **global warming** and **climate change**.

8

Plants have a short growing season in the tundra—the shortest on the planet. It's only about 50 days long, shorter than a summer break from school.

With chilly soil and little time, how do plants grow? Many plants, such as grasses, lichens, mosses, and shrubs, stay small. They hug the ground to avoid bitter winds.

Close to the ground, short plants absorb the sun's heat radiating from the soil. Their shallow roots draw moisture from the active layer above the permafrost.

The purple saxifrage flower of Denali, Alaska, is adapted for its inhospitable environment. One of the first tundra flowers to bloom when temperatures warm up, it often makes its cheery appearance as the snow melts.

This cushion plant grows in a ground-hugging cluster that looks like a pillow. It sets down roots in crevices between rocks, which absorb the sun's energy.

Did You Know?

The Inuit people of the Arctic eat the purple saxifrage's sweet, starshaped blossoms.

Animals Living in the

Food is scarce during frigid tundra winters when snow covers the landscape. Many animals survive by **migrating** to warmer climates. Immense herds of lichen-loving caribou move south to forest biomes.

Animals such as the singing vole, named because of the shrill noise it makes when it spots **predators**, thrive in the **subnivian layer**. There they can nibble on roots and stems. Some animals **hibernate**, like the Arctic ground squirrel and the grizzly bear.

What Eats What?

Caribou are **herbivores** that eat moss and lichen. Grizzly bears are **omnivores** that eat both plants and small animals. Large predators, including wolves and polar bears, are **carnivores** that eat caribou, seals, and other animals.

Tundra Have Adapted

Other animals stay outside and brave the elements. Polar bears, seals, and walruses depend on **blubber** and thick coats to protect them against the cold, both on the land and in the water.

Words to Know

migrate: to move from one environment to another when seasons change.

predator: an animal that hunts another animal for food.

subnivian layer: the area below a layer of snow and above the soil.

hibernate: to sleep through the winter in a cave or underground.

blubber: a thick layer of fat beneath the skin that provides insulation for tundra dwellers.

herbivore: an animal that eats only plants.

omnivore: an animal that eats both plants and animals.

carnivore: an animal that eats only other animals.

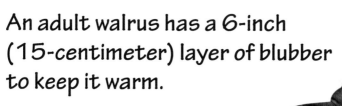

An adult walrus has a 6-inch (15-centimeter) layer of blubber to keep it warm.

Its two hanging tusks act as built-in pick-axes. Walruses stab their tusks into the ice to hoist themselves out of the water and to haul their blubbery bodies over their rocky, icy habitat.

Other adaptations include bigger bodies, shorter legs, and smaller ears. This is a combination that helps many Arctic mammals and birds survive.

here: The Arctic hare has short ears to conserve heat.

there: The jackrabbit of the desert biome has oversized ears to allow heat to escape.

To blend into the background of the snowy environment, the Arctic hare turns from a gray color in the summer to white in the winter. This is called camouflage.

The Arctic fox, ermine, and willow ptarmigan also turn white in the winter.

Did You Know?

The Arctic tern migrates the longest distance of any bird—21,750 miles (35,000 kilometers), from the Arctic to Antarctica and back again! The journey takes about 3 months.

14

Environmental Threats

Today, the tundra faces many threats.

Oil drilling causes air, land, water, and noise pollution. The tundra is a sensitive environment. Buildings, roads, and pipelines put pressure and heat on the landscape, melting the permafrost.

Oil spills are disastrous, ruining the environment and killing animals on land and in the water.

Slick oil covers skin, fur, and feathers. Animals' natural abilities to fly and to remain insulated and waterproof fail, so they freeze to death or drown. When sea birds, harbor seals, and otters try to lick themselves clean, they swallow toxic oil.

Oily waters poison salmon, whales, and bears.

Global warming and climate change have impacted the tundra more than any other place on the planet. The earth's higher temperatures are causing Arctic and Antarctic ice to melt and **glaciers** to shrink. If all the earth's glaciers and ice sheets completely melted, sea levels would rise about 200 feet (61 meters)!

Thaw depth of the permafrost has also increased, causing dead plants and animals in the soil to break down.

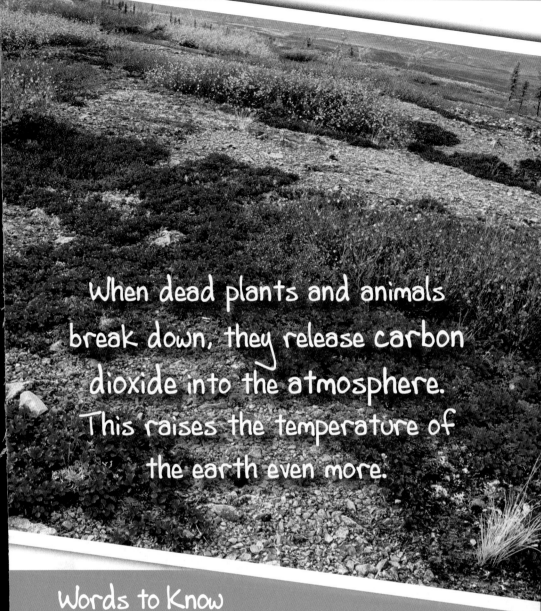

When dead plants and animals break down, they release carbon dioxide into the atmosphere. This raises the temperature of the earth even more.

Words to Know

glacier: an enormous mass of frozen snow and ice that moves across the earth's surface.

carbon dioxide: a greenhouse gas that contributes to global warming and climate chage.

atmosphere: the mixture of gases that surround a planet.

Biodiversity at Risk

Many plants and animals are at risk in the tundra. And when an animal or plant **species** becomes extinct, that means it's gone forever. There are many causes of **extinction**. Natural occurrences, such as volcanic eruptions, have caused extinctions in the past.

Today, destruction of habitat and food sources is the largest threat to animal biodiversity. If the permafrost melts too much, it will change the balance of the ecosystem and what plant and animal species can live there.

Because of climate change, polar bears struggle to find enough food to survive. Sometimes mother polar bears are so thin they can't produce enough milk to feed their young.

Many bears have attempted to swim great distances in search of food. Sadly, some drown in the process.

In 2008 the United States government named the polar bear an endangered species. There's a real possibility that this symbol of the Arctic could become extinct in your lifetime.

Words to Know

species: a type of animal or plant.

extinction: the death of an entire species so that it no longer exists.

Did You Know?

In the summer of 2008, people in Iceland spotted polar bears that had ventured 200 miles (322 kilometers) from their home turf to hunt for seals. It's a sign that climate change has caused the polar bears to roam greater distances in search of food.

Path to Extinction

Rare: Only a small number of the species is alive. Scientists are concerned about the future of the species.

Threatened: The species lives, but its numbers will likely continue to decline. It will probably become endangered.

Endangered: The species is in danger of extinction in the very near future.

Extinct in the Wild: Some members of the species live, but only in protected captivity and not out in the wild.

Extinct: The species has completely died out. It has disappeared from the planet.

The Future of the

In the last 100 years, the earth's temperature has risen by more than 1 degree Fahrenheit. Sounds pretty small, doesn't it? However, the impact of just that 1 degree is enormous. And the temperature is rising faster than ever before.

Many scientists fear that global warming may eliminate Arctic regions, including the tundra, forever. Shorter winters and longer summers will mean more melting of snow cover and melting deeper into the permafrost. Plants will die, animal migrating patterns will change, and the tundra biome as we know it could be gone.

The overall effect that global warming will have on the tundra is still uncertain. What we do know is that the tundra is the most fragile biome, and it will be the first to reflect any change in the earth's climate.

Tundra

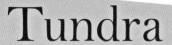

The global rise in temperature
will damage the sensitive
environment of the tundra more
than any other biome.

Conservation Challenge

Think about what You can do to benefit the environment. What actions can you take? How can you inspire others to do the same?

- Reduce your carbon footprint. That's the impact your activities have on the environment when they produce carbon dioxide. Walk, pedal your bike, or ride your skateboard when possible. It's good for your body and the environment.

When traveling longer distances, take the bus or help your family organize a carpool.

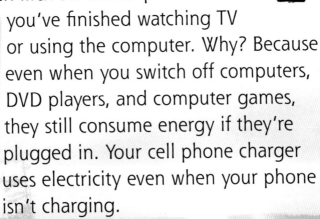

- Switch off the lights when you leave a room. Turn off all electronics when you're finished using them. When you enter and leave your house, shut the door quickly. The furnace or air conditioner will require less energy to do its job.

- Plug electronics into a single power strip. Then flick off the strip when you've finished watching TV or using the computer. Why? Because even when you switch off computers, DVD players, and computer games, they still consume energy if they're plugged in. Your cell phone charger uses electricity even when your phone isn't charging.

These "energy vampires" endlessly guzzle electricity, 24/7.

Glossary

active layer: the layer of soil that melts in the summer.

adapt: changes a plant or animal makes to survive in new or different conditions.

adaptation: the development of physical or behavioral changes to survive in an environment.

atmosphere: the mixture of gases that surround a planet.

biodiversity: the range of living things in an ecosystem.

biome: a large natural area with a distinctive climate, geology, and set of water resources. A biome's plants and animals are adapted for life there.

blubber: a thick layer of fat beneath the skin that provides insulation for tundra dwellers.

carbon dioxide: a greenhouse gas that contributes to global warming and climate change.

carbon footprint: the direct effect an individual's actions and lifestyle have on the environment in terms of carbon dioxide emissions, which contribute to global warming.

carnivore: an animal that eats only other animals.

climate: average weather patterns in an area over a period of many years.

climate change: a change in the world's weather and climate.

ecosystem: a community of living and nonliving things and their environment. Living things are plants, animals, and insects. Nonliving things are soil, rocks, and water.

Glossary

environment: everything in nature, living and nonliving.

extinction: the death of an entire species so that it no longer exists.

food chain: a community of animals and plants where each is eaten by another higher up in the chain.

geology: the rocks, minerals, and physical structure of an area.

glacier: an enormous mass of frozen snow and ice that moves across the earth's surface.

global warming: the gradual warming of the planet, causing climate change.

habitat: a plant or animal's home.

herbivore: an animal that eats only plants.

hibernate: to sleep through the winter in a cave or underground.

migrate: to move from one environment to another when seasons change.

Northern Hemisphere: the half of the earth north of the equator.

omnivore: an animal that eats both plants and animals.

permafrost: the tundra's permanently frozen layer of soil just beneath the surface of the ground.

predator: an animal that hunts another animal for food.

species: a type of animal or plant.

subnivian layer: the area below a layer of snow and above the soil.

timberline: also called the treeline. How far north or how high in the mountains trees grow.

Further Investigations

Cherry, Lynn. *How We Know What We Know About Our Changing Climate: Scientists and Kids Explore Global Warming.* Dawn Publications, 2008.

Latham, Donna. *Amazing Biome Projects You Can Build Yourself.* Nomad Press, 2009.

Reilly, Kathleen M. *Planet Earth: 25 Environmental Projects You Can Build Yourself.* Nomad Press, 2008.

Rothschild, David. *Earth Matters: An Encyclopedia of Ecology.* DK Publishing, 2008.

Smithsonian Institution National Museum of Natural History
www.mnh.si.edu
Washington, D.C.

US National Parks www.us-parks.com

Enchanted Learning, Biomes
www.enchantedlearning.com/biomes

Energy Efficiency and Renewable Energy
www.eere.energy.gov/kids

Geography for Kids www.kidsgeo.com

Inch in a Pinch: Saving the Earth
www.inchinapinch.com

Kids Do Ecology
www.kids.nceas.ucsb.edu

Library ThinkQuest
www.thinkquest.org

National Geographic Kids
www.kids.nationalgeographic.com

NOAA for Kids
www.oceanservice.noaa.gov/kids

Oceans for Youth
www.oceansforyouth.org

The Nature Conservancy
www.nature.org

World Wildlife Federation
www.panda.org

Index

adaptations, 7, 9-10, 11-14
animals, 6, 11-14, 15-16, 19-22, 23
Arctic hare, 14
Arctic tern, 14
bears, 11, 12, 16, 20-21
biodiversity, 3, 19-22
biomes, 1-2
caribou, 11
climate change, 8, 17-18, 21, 23-24
conservation, 25-26
environmental issues, 15-18, 19, 21, 23-26

extinction, 19-20, 22
food/food chain, 7-8, 11, 19-21
future of tundra, 23-24
global warming, 8, 17-18, 21, 23-24
humans, impact of, 15-18, 25-26
migration, 11, 14, 23
oil drilling/oil spills, 15-16
permafrost, 5-6, 8, 15, 17, 19, 23
plants, 6, 7-10, 19, 23

polar bears, 12, 16, 20-21
rainfall, 3, 7
seasons, 3, 5-6, 9-12, 14
singing voles, 11
soil, 3, 5-6, 7, 9. *See also* permafrost
sun/sunlight, 9, 10
temperature, 3, 11-12, 17-18, 23-24. *See also* global warming
walruses, 12, 13